IN THE CITY

by Kathryn E. Lewis
illustrated by Tatjana Krizmanic

Orlando Boston Dallas Chicago San Diego

Visit *The Learning Site!*
www.harcourtschool.com

I can see an
apartment building.

I can see a bus.

I can see a subway train.

I can see a park.

I can see a cab.

I can see a
skyscraper.

I can see the
whole city!